The Wealthy Consultant

The Wealthy Consultant
Confessions of a 9-Figure Advisor

Taylor A. Welch

Published in the United States by Game Changer Publishing:
www.GameChangerPublishing.com

Illustrations by Kristen McCall
KristenMcCall.com

Paperback ISBN: ISBN: 978-1-961189-60-7
Hardcover ISBN: ISBN: 978-1-961189-61-4
Digital: ISBN: 978-1-961189-59-1

1st edition, July 2023
Printed in the United States of America

Read This First!

Just to say thanks for buying and reading my book, I would like to give you a few free bonus gifts, no strings attached.

Download Your Free Gifts Now:

The Wealthy Consultant

Confessions of a 9-Figure Advisor

Taylor A. Welch

www.GameChangerPublishing.com

Table of Contents

Introduction

Introductions are mostly a waste of time.

I'm sorry other authors make you go through all that.

I'm not going to waste your time. Let's dive right in.

CHAPTER 1

How We Got Here

*"What I fear is not the enemy's strategy
but our own mistakes."* - Pericles

I build and scale businesses for a living, all kinds of businesses, but mostly consulting, training, E-learning, and continued education. The models you are going to learn work predictably and safely, but there are nuances – I will teach you those nuances.

If you're a consultant, an expert, or a coach, you sell information; you sell something technically invisible. You sell a result, an outcome, a lesson, an experience, or a piece of wisdom. You sell something that cannot be put into a box and shipped out via FedEx. You sell something that doesn't drive or have four wheels, nor can it be operated like you would operate a toy or a motorbike.

But if you're good at what you do, and that's who this book is for, consultants, coaches, and experts, who are legitimately good at what they do, then what you sell is far more powerful than a vehicle, a house, or a motorboat. It's your experience and expertise that move the human species forward.

When humans invented the ability to write, we jumped a few levels in the cosmic pecking order. Suddenly, we could pass along our lessons from generation to generation. Consider this book one of my contributions to your evolutionary advancement. I want to teach you how to scale your business's impact on society, even as I scale your income.

As you read this book, I want you to feel:

- Certain
- Methodical
- Well planned
- Structured
- Excited
- Enthusiastic

I do not want you to feel:

- Stressed
- Nervous
- Anxious
- Afraid
- Vulnerable

I want to turn you away from "scale at all costs" and point you toward controlled, organized, measured growth. As we travel this journey, we will learn the secrets that underlie the world's most successful, secure, defensible companies.

The Hamster Wheel Sucks

A client roster in the thousands has taught me some things. Mostly everyone is busy running up and down a hamster wheel.

The only way they can continue growth is to sell more clients this month than last. Then next month, they do it all over again. Your burnout is inevitable if you're not armed with the methodologies in this book. Even if you figure out some things to make it "work," it will not work sustainably until you ditch the "side gig" mentality and build a real business around what you do.

Real businesses create enterprise value. You cannot sell a "client roster" if that client roster depends entirely on you. The more crucial you are to your business's success, the lower your business's value will be. This doesn't mean you cannot be heavily involved in your company. You should be involved for as long as you want, especially at the beginning.

I am an advocate of optionality. Risk mitigation is not about being "risk-free." It's about creating and securing optionality so the risks cannot hurt you as much as they otherwise would. When you are single-source dependent, we call it "concentration risk." Most experts, consultants, and trainers have concentration risk riddled throughout their business like a body full of cancer. This book will teach you how to fix all of that, and I believe if you implement my principles, this will be one of the best investments you will ever make.

CHAPTER 2

Three Keys to Scaling a Business

"Reputation is the cornerstone of power. Make your reputation unassailable." - Robert Greene

Definition of Scale

So let's start with a definition of scale. Because this is a book about scale, most people don't realize that scale does not just mean "more growth."

I view scale as a rebalancing of the size of your business against your total addressable market (TAM). Scale is a breaking of homeostasis that pushes your market share up, usually against significant resistance and pressure. When your revenues break the normal and natural pace of growth and instead jump into "scale" territory, you go from being in the flow of traffic to breaking out of the flow of traffic. As speed increases, so can the danger.

Bad scale is anything that violates the safety threshold of the business. To put this into perspective, let's define bad scale as anything that blows past the natural "market cap" of a business without proper protections. I don't mean market cap the way you would define a publicly traded company. Instead, market cap here refers to the business' risk threshold. The market cap of a business is that threshold where anything beyond that compromises the safety of the business to the point of diminishing returns.

There are ways to make money in a consulting business that are so dangerous they are undesirable. A business using the internet must honor its "market cap," which makes this challenging because the market cap is constantly changing. As you staff up or fix systems or infrastructure, you might push that market cap threshold higher, and scale becomes less dangerous. Then, if you get close to that market cap and cross it, things become risky again.

This is a mouthful, so let me explain in more detail. A business enterprise comprises people, systems, and intellectual property. You find finances, bank accounts, and expense accounts inside these systems. When we sit down to define how a business is valued, we come up with three things, and I'm drastically oversimplifying this here for the sake of quick information transfer, but this is the general simplification:

- Cash (or assets)
- Cash flows (current)
- Future cash flows

Your future cash flows are always discounted because they haven't happened yet. The term "discounted cash flow" is commonly used in private equity to answer the question, "What are we willing to pay now for the likelihood of cash flows in the future?"

Future cash flow comes down to a lot of different variables.

- Supply and demand
- Customer acquisition
- Retention
- Brand and reputation
- Receivables
- Team and people
- Etcetera

People often become confused by the fact that a business's future cash flow has much more to it than "Can I acquire new clients or customers?" Your valuations will not come from your ability to get new customers. Instead, your valuation will come from how *many ways* you can get new customers. It's the diversity here that maximizes your multiple. Why is this? Because when people buy a business, they're looking for certainty. Ten ways to grow a business is more "certain" than only one way to grow a business. It's more of a question of certainty of future cash flow than the amount of future cash flow.

Anybody can "hack" the volume game. You can acquire customers and then immediately refund them. People aren't going to pay for that. The debits and credits would cross each other out on the P&L. **So, the definition of unhealthy scale for me is when the growth of the business violates the certainty of the future of the business.**

When I say "market cap," I'm referencing that line in the sand where everything beyond compromises the safety of the business's future. We don't charge mindlessly past that; we fix the business, and in doing so, we push the line higher, then we advance. Anything that compromises or throws uncertainty on whether your business can fulfill its future promises is a bad move. Don't do it.

The reason this is so important is because, again, "scale" is easy if the definition is "growth" or "fast growth." The good scale protects the reputation as it grows. You want to turn the growth of your business into a multiplier. As the business grows, it becomes more respected and better trusted. A lot of businesses get this backward. They will attempt to grow the size of the business by harvesting all of the goodwill in their market. This is eating from tomorrow in order to hit an arbitrary number today.

No matter how large or small you are, there is unharvested, latent "goodwill" or trust in your market. People have seen your content, but they haven't purchased your products yet. They've listened to your ads or podcasts but haven't become clients. This is a good thing. You've likely heard the term "moat" before. Charlie Munger talks about business moats often. The moat is what protects you from competition. It protects you from being stolen from. It keeps you safer from incumbents and creates 'barriers of entry' when someone wants to talk to or sell to your market.

Well, think about it this way. Your market's unconverted goodwill acts as a "moat" against others who do what you do. One of the best moats for training and consulting companies are the people who have subscribed, listened to and implemented your advice and feedback but have not yet given you money. They are listening to you because of your content, and the more they listen, the more "bought-in" they become on their way to becoming buyers. Most people think, "How can I get those people to hurry up and convert into clients and customers?" But you cannot (and should not) sacrifice the future reputation of your company to scale faster now. This is the equivalent of robbing tomorrow to pay a hungry monster today.

Leveraging Your Brand and Reputation

If you do this too long, you'll end up where I was the first time. Too many "tomorrows" into your future, and you'll be unable to keep kicking the can down the road. Your reputation is more important than a few extra dollars collected too early. So, a business that scales past its ability to protect and improve its reputation is a business that has violated and gone beyond its market cap. This is when the scale turns ugly.

The bigger you get, the more inspired people are in your market; the more loved and respected your brand is. This is a good scale. There are levers we can build into the business so growth, rather than "harvesting" goodwill, instead multiplies goodwill. These levers come down to a simple idea known as "leverage." We aren't going to scale through addition; we will scale through multiplication. This is an idea that will change the way you think about growth. Whether you're running a business in consulting, training, education, software, laundromats, physical/tangible goods, or done-for-you services, the size and scope don't matter. What matters is this: do you have enough leverage to grow exponentially without sacrificing goodwill and reputation?

Three Types of Leverage

There are different kinds of leverage, but the main three from my experience are as follows:

- Financial
- Operational
- Brand

Each of these three pieces of leverage provides different advantages to the business. For example, financial leverage is getting something you did not pay for. Think business credit, lines of credit, even mortgages – all examples of financial leverage. Operational leverage is getting something you did not work for. Brand leverage is getting access to people you would've had no previous way of talking to. Brand is incredible because it's when your reputation begins to precede you. People you've never met or talked to will feel a certain way about you simply because of the leverage built into your brand.

Our goal is to build leverage into the business in as many ways as possible. When you have leverage, you can grow without the traditional "trade-offs" most businesses experience. Your "yield" outpaces your inputs. So, with that said, in this chapter, I want to share with you three of the leading models we install to create scale via leverage.

The First is Attention

Attention is your ability to go out and get the eyes and ears of a group of people without working linearly for it. Attention is not cheap. Attention is expensive and only getting more expensive. Some of the brightest minds today say that oil is the old guard's currency and attention is the new guard's currency. When you can go out and command the eyes and ears of 100 million people, you can parlay or arbitrage that attention into whatever business you want to grow or scale.

Attention is the leverage of media. This is the first way you can scale a brand or a business without eating into your future goodwill because the more attention you accumulate, the more productive everything in your business will become.

Now if we split attention into sub-components, you have to get good at two things. The first is "getting attention." This is done through advertising or content. Publishing products or books (such as this one), videos, podcasts, webinars, emails, billboards, etc., is how you begin accumulating the leverage of attention.

The "getting attention" is usually done by paying money in exchange for someone else's audience. You send money to social media networks or advertise to someone's email list or podcast, and bam, you've secured the attention of a group of people who did not know you. You can also do it the long tail way by publishing great content and having people find you organically.

Attention Retention

After you have secured the attention, the second piece of attention is "retaining the attention." You keep or retain this attention by providing good material consistently for people to pay attention to. Take this book, for example. You're reading this book. Someone on one of my teams probably paid for an ad for you to see the book. Or, maybe you heard about it from a friend. Maybe you saw it on my socials. All of these are different forms and mediums of attention or media.

The first battle was to get enough of your attention so that you would download the book. That has been done successfully — +1 for me. The second part is more arduous, more complicated, and more important, and that is the keeping of your attention. Through the keeping of your intention, the accrual of your trust begins.

If I spend money — let's say I put something in front of you and get your attention — but then I waste it, you will never give me your attention again. However, if I put something in front of you, and your attention is well rewarded — you begin to think, "This is life-changing, this is incredible" — this is where I begin to transfer value in exchange for your trust. I've succeeded in keeping your attention. This is all in the context of advertising, content, and marketing – for the record. Your consulting, education, coaching or training company cannot grow without securing the attention of the people who trust you.

Securing attention is part one, and keeping and stewarding that attention is part two. At this point, you have converted someone's attention that you had to pay for into trust that you get to now steward properly.

You cannot hack or trick your way into keeping someone's attention, at least not the good kind of attention. You must be worthy of keeping it.

Repeat Customers

The second point of leverage is the retention of the customer or client. Let's say that I spent $10,000 to get attention. Of the people who pay attention, 70 people give me money to buy a product or a book. That's a cost per acquisition (CPA) of $142. Then let's say I steward that attention properly, and they think, *Amazing value. What else can I buy?* The minute they buy the second product is when the real business begins.

At that point, I've not only kept their attention, but I've also retained a customer or a client, and the acquisition cost of the second purchase is not $142, or even half of $142; it's zero. If your products are great, someone will buy one thing from you and then buy another and another and another. These are called repeat customers. The better your products are, the better your services are, and the more repeat customers you will have.

When you see big organizations scaling, putting together infrastructure, new products, and new opportunities and partnerships, you're witnessing a company that has likely decreased its acquisition costs through outstanding products and services. Their acquisition costs decreased, so they can now re-invest the extra profits into building more moats in their business. They've arbitraged the extra money on their P&L right back into the company. This is leverage at its finest. Other companies cannot compete because they cannot afford to. This is a moat.

Some businesses get retention down and can use retention to create network effects. We're not going to talk about network effects in this book. However, you need to understand that a network effect is when whatever you're selling gets more valuable the bigger your network gets. We don't typically see network effects as a significant lever in consulting or training companies. However, network effects are a form of leverage if you have software attached to your company or some community element.

If you want to scale your company, the third common lever is pricing. Pricing is a strategic needle mover, and it's more than your pricing. I'm talking about pricing models.

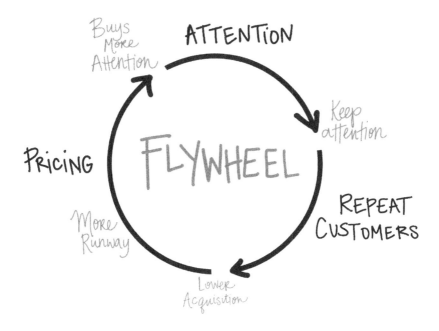

Cash Flow Conversion Cycles

What I've found with most people is a mismatch between their pricing & their long-term goals. Their pricing is too high, too low, or their pricing model is just plain incorrect. There is more that goes into pricing than we can cover in a short book like this. Some people have subscription models and need more upfront fees. Some have ridiculous upfront fees but no recurring or what I call "revolving" pricing. It comes down to your cash conversion cycles (CCC) and the ultimate end goal for the business. For instance, if you hope to exit one day, the buyer will look at your discounted future cash flow. This means you should have some receivables to show an aging report. Receivables show the amount of money you've already secured but have not yet collected.

Again, pricing is unique and custom, and I can't prescribe anything in a book format without talking to you first. Here's a quick story that might give some great examples. I went into a bank once and asked for a line of credit, and they asked for an aging report. I said, "What's an aging report?"

They said, "We need to see your receivables."

We had no receivables; we collected 100% of everything upfront. I thought this was good, but the bank immediately said, "Great, there's no future cash flow here. It's a zero-dollar runway." No line of credit. This was in 2018 and my businesses had just begun to really grow. This important lesson taught me the value of recurring revenue – or a recurring "book" of business. Regarding pricing, your cash conversion cycle is a big deal, as your price will ultimately come down to the end goal. We want to use pricing as a "lever" that can predict and control the revenues coming into a business.

When you get these three things dialed in — attention, retention, and pricing — scale is a lot easier.

Your attention becomes cheap (or free). Your retention is high, your churn is low, and you have a business that collects and creates cash flow for the future. At this point, you are sustainable enough to afford to scale the right way.

Pricing provides a vast advantage that allows you to begin taking advantage of your competition.

CHAPTER 3

How To Scale With Product

"Where a finite-minded player makes products they think they can sell to people, the infinite-minded player makes products that people want to buy. The former is primarily focused on how the sale of those products benefits the company; the latter is primarily focused on how the products benefit those who buy them." - Simon Sinek

Diversifying Product Offerings

In this chapter, I want to get into some of the different forms of products you can use. This chapter will diversify the way your business makes money.

This is important because businesses that only have one product offering are the fastest to die from the competition. Let's look at it this way. When you look at buying a new home, there are cheap and expensive homes. Different types of buyers build different types of homes. In the automobile market, there are cheap cars and expensive cars. Different manufacturers build different kinds of cars.

Some manufacturers build cheap cars and expensive cars within the same brand. Why is that? Because there is a vertical in every "total addressable market" (TAM). A vertical is a collection of buyers in a similar industry. If you are going to scale, at some point, you must also decide to go "vertical," which means you will start servicing customers and clients at different stages inside the industry's product suite. This requires you to evolve from a "one trick pony" or a "one-hit wonder" into a resilient and durable business model.

Deliverable vs. Monetization

When you peel back the layers of just about every consulting, training, or education company in the world, we see three main types of products inside the business. Later in the book, we will tackle a different subject — monetization. Monetization and productization are different. Think of "products" as a deliverable. Think of monetization as the payment you collect or how the person is giving you money

What happens when someone swipes their card or sends a wire to buy something?

They are buying a "receivable," and you are selling a "deliverable." An exchange happens, with money transferred in the middle. There are three primary types of deliverables we build in the training & consulting industry.

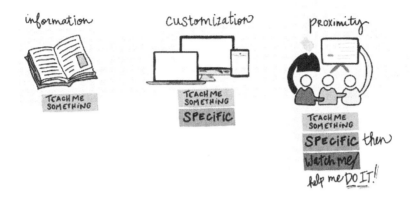

Information

The first type of product is information. This might seem basic or "duh," but that's because most principles are fundamental (we overlook them). Information, or "knowledge," forms a bedrock for you. If you're going to scale a firm, there should be ample information surrounding your brand that makes people's lives better.

An excellent example, again, would be this book. You bought it somewhere, and now you're reading it. The more you read, the more your business will grow and the happier you will become. Hopefully, you're receiving more value from the book's contents than the money you spent to acquire it. Millions of people receive information from me and my companies, and the consensus is always the same. "I can't believe I only paid $$ for this." That's a good market sentiment to build. You don't want to overprice your information.

Some great thinkers and practitioners today give all of their information away. Let's talk about that.

Free vs. Cheap

I value you, but I won't give you all my best work for free. The common denominator among all successful people is that they paid to be there. Sometimes we pay in money (currency), and sometimes, we pay in "sweat equity" (another form of currency), but we all pay to be there.

When something is free, you will receive a lot of respect and goodwill from it. When something is expensive, you will receive a lot of commitment from the buyer. I like to have products all along the spectrum because I'm balancing two conflicting goals for you if you're reading this book:

1. Consuming the information
2. Implementing the information

Many things are downloaded or "saved" on social media and never consumed or implemented. I'm offsetting some of that by making people pay something to access the information.

At some point, your market must pay you for information, or else the cycle is incomplete. If you give everything away for free, you are leaving a massive hole in the conversion cycle of a market. People don't want everything for free. They value things that they pay for.

That said, I still publish a lot of training and information for free because I have to transfer material to my audience so that we all become more wealthy, prosperous, and autonomous together. You can find this content everywhere, but there's a list of resources at the end of this book.

Why Information is Cheap

There are thousands of people like you reading this book. The same information, the same medium. Information can be cheap because it's affordable to produce, cost-effective for the consumer, and not customized to the individual.

Information is designed to transfer facts, data, and perspectives simultaneously to many people. If information becomes too expensive, it will be non-transferable. This would harm civilization because people would not move forward. So, our job as a species is to democratize information and deflate the cost of acquiring new skills and tools across all industries.

Customization

So, information comes first; if you do not publish information for free or cheap, you will struggle to own a vertical. The second form of a product is customization.

If you look up a Jordan Peterson video, you will find a video with millions of views. It's changing everyone's life based on their perception of the information. The information isn't being customized, it's just being displayed, and people are customizing it for themselves. When you get into consulting or training, your second level of a product usually customizes the information for the client.

Here's an example:

For one of my training platforms, *wealthyconsultant.com*, we have a lot of information. People buy and consume the information; usually, these range from $10 to $100, but sometimes higher depending on the product. These are books, courses, and newsletters.

Eventually, you get to the level where you're wanting extra support. Think about it like this: you must take out an insurance policy for your vehicle because you want to be protected if something goes wrong. People do the same with information. They ask, "How do I "insure" this purchase??" If you're looking for ways to maximize your chances of success, the answer to that is usually customization.

You do not want information, knowledge, or education at this level; you want to know *what should I NOT do.* What do I narrow in on to achieve my outcome?

At the information level, you are searching to learn how the world works. At the customization level, you're searching for how YOUR world should look based on the outcomes you want to see. People pay extra for customization. A common mistake is when people believe the price is correlated to the number of materials in the product. This is not true.

The price increases in proportion to the specificity of the product. People will pay more for less "stuff" if it's more relevant or appropriate.

Time is an asset none of us get more of, so think of customization as spending more money to save more time.

Proximity

Level three is access and proximity.

This is where the "guru model" came from. You will notice a multiplicative effect when you build the brand level required to scale anything. As your attention grows, more and more people will get value from being around you. This is where masterminds come into play. The original mastermind was Thomas Edison and Henry Ford, getting groups of people together who were smart.

There was a convention years ago where Albert Einstein gathered 20 or so scientists, and they essentially discovered "quantum physics." Masterminds create proximity. Some people pay multiple six figures each year for access to other like minded people – just to absorb their thinking, ask them questions, and learn from their perspectives.

You might read this and think, *Holy cow, why in the world would you pay six figures just to be around somebody?* Often, one idea can be worth millions of dollars. If you are going purely by the merit of one good idea, imagine having 10, 15, or 20 good ideas that can each create millions of dollars of wealth by implementation. Masterminds and mentors can be a conduit to generate these ideas.

Imagine 200 or 300 years ago if you could engage with John J. Hill or Cornelius Vanderbilt. These people built the railroads and created billions of dollars in enterprise value. J. Hill was one of the most successful railroad operators in history. John D. Rockefeller mastered finance and operations to a level nobody alive on planet Earth had mastered while he was alive.

Imagine being able to sit down with them and ask them questions.

- How do you decide what to study?
- Why are you fighting with JP Morgan?
- How do you get excited in the morning?
- What do you think about competition and distribution?

These are things I would have paid a lot of money for!

It wasn't possible. One time someone said, "I hate masterminds. I just don't like the idea of paying to be someone's friend." I thought, *I'm glad I could pay to be someone's friend because I would never have met them if I couldn't!*

I pay mentors happily and gladly because I get to tap into years of learning, often avoiding the mistakes they made in the process.

Summary

If we summarize the three levels, here is what we get:

1. Teach me something.
2. Teach me something specific.
3. Teach me something specific, then watch me / help me do it.

CHAPTER 4

Eight Figure Teams

"The weaker the culture, the more leaders must rely on policies and procedures to make people behave in a certain way. What you lack in culture, you must make up for in legislation." - John Maxwell

Outsourcing Your Time and Work

One of the biggest multipliers for growing your company is the people you trust to get the work done.

My experience in building teams started many years ago when hiring my first team member. My small business was doing wonderfully well, and suddenly I found myself stuck between a rock and a hard place. I was uniquely situated and capable of growing, but I had no time to handle the extra growth. Every week, a giant portion of my week was filled with arduous labor I didn't enjoy performing.

The business was throttled because I had no time to make it bigger. When I took new clients or won new business, I would spend all my time servicing the business and couldn't *run* the business. This might be a position you've found yourself in, but you must know the issue is never time; it only feels that way. The issue is what you are doing with the time you have. More specifically, to fix this, we need to remove things you're currently doing that you do not enjoy and replace these activities with activities you're uniquely capable of doing well.

To do this, you need a team.

There are plenty of good books about managing time. My friend Dan Martell has an incredible book that will show you how to *Buy Back Your Time*. It's an in-depth training guide for mastering time allocation. He is a pro, and his recipes work consistently. I assume you have the means and resources to learn how to manage your time elsewhere, so the issue I'll cover in this chapter isn't time management. It's people management. If you don't feel you have the time to do what you want, it can usually be traced back to a team or personnel issue.

Two Types of Outsourcing

Scaling a consulting business without a good team is a path to burnout. You can't scale if you do not have the right team. There are two key levels of outsourcing you will need to learn how to do if you're going to scale a consulting firm.

The First is Outsourcing Labor

Outsourcing labor means finding someone who can push the buttons, schedule the meetings, and do the work. We're outsourcing our "hands" at this level. This can be an itemized list of "to-do" work you give to an assistant or a 1099 contractor. It can be administrative duties you give an executive or virtual assistant. It's effective, but it will not allow you to scale.

The Second Type of Outsourcing is Outsourcing Your Decisions

This goes beyond the realm of your hands and into the realm of your brain. You're replacing or duplicating your mind.

When you get people around you who can duplicate your thinking, decisions, and strategic responsibilities, your world opens up, and you can take on much more at the same time.

I am grateful to be surrounded by incredible staff and people. These people can create new partnerships, relationships, and products and even make company-wide directional choices that enable us to grow, sometimes without my direct involvement.

When you can do this, the previous limitations slowly dissolve because you no longer have to use your time and bandwidth for every little thing. This is why time management is not the real issue. Time is not your most valuable asset. Your most valuable asset is your energy or your bandwidth. People like Tim Cook, Elon Musk, and the President of the United States – all of them use this principle so they can accomplish more. There is no way the President can be involved in every single decision in the country. The cabinet, advisors, and staff are all hired to provide insights, and in some instances make decisions so the show can keep moving.

Your ability to guard, steward, and direct energy will either propel your growth potential, or it will cap you way beneath your potential. So how do you go from managing time to managing energy? How do we go from managing tasks and labor to managing bandwidth and strategic, long-term direction?

The key is to create an effective team, which you will learn how to do in this chapter. There are four key responsibilities you have if you're going to build an effective team and scale your company through people

All leaders must do four things to build a robust, healthy team of thinkers and decision-makers.

- Hire
- Train
- Equip
- Trust

First, you have to hire them. This sounds obvious, but it's worth learning how to do it. There's a book called *Who*, by Geoff Smart that will show you how to use "top grading" to find great talent. But later in this chapter, I'm going to give you a simpler model to rate & score your talent before you bring them in. When I teach this to people live or in workshops, I'm always surprised that people haven't built a team because they're just afraid to hire the first person. You have to hire to get good at hiring.

Second, you need to train them.

Third, you must equip them. This is different from training them. Training involves developing competency; equipping involves giving autonomy and decision-making authority. It's possible for someone to be trained well and then micromanaged to a degree they cannot do their job. Be careful because if you equip someone and they do not move the organization forward, you must replace them.

Fourth, you must trust them. The greatest investment you can make into your team is how you handle their mistakes. Everyone will make mistakes, there's no such thing as perfect. We do, however, eliminate *repeat* mistakes in the same areas of competency. Your leaders should be failing forward, but they should never be failing at the same things over and over again.

There's a story about the CEO of IBM that I like. An executive had made a bad decision, resulting in a multi-million-dollar loss for the company. The executive approached the CEO and offered their resignation. The CEO replied, "I don't accept this resignation. I've invested several million dollars into you; to prevent us from making this mistake again. Learn from it, and let's go forward."

This is an excellent example of trusting your team even when they get it wrong.

3 Levels to Replace

I've learned to live in the tension of these principles. It is not always easy, but we must all eventually remove ourselves from even the things we're great at. There is no way to scale if you are responsible for everything.

The first level you should outsource is obvious. You want to replace yourself with the things you're not good at and don't enjoy. Everybody starts here, and it's the lowest-hanging fruit.

The second level is less obvious, and that is replacing yourself with things you're good at but don't enjoy. There are plenty of activities you're likely doing now because you need to do them. Perhaps you've become good at them, but they don't excite you or get you fired up when you think about them. You should eventually replace these activities. What you'll notice when you do this is that those areas will improve dramatically. Why? Because we don't often *master* what we don't enjoy. Somewhere in the world, there's a person who loves to do what you're good at but you don't love to do it. They will come in and immediately make it better.

The third level is the hardest. You must replace yourself with what you're both good at and enjoy doing, but you're not irreplaceable at. This is a requirement. You must get to the place where the lion's share of your time is spent doing things you cannot be replaced at. Only you can do them. Only you can do them the way you do them. This requires you to replace yourself everywhere you are *not* irreplaceable.

There are likely 2 or 3 activities that you can do better than anyone else in the world. You have to find them. When you do them, you feel like you will live forever. Nobody understands how you do them so well, and honestly, you don't either. You can't explain breathing to a plant; you just breathe. Your zone of genius is like that. It's where you can demonstrate such a high level of excellence that people stop and watch when they see your work.

Here's what you might notice about this chapter. We are riddled with limiting beliefs regarding people. It doesn't start with others; it starts with us. If you believe you must "work hard" to make money, you will naturally rig your environment so you're doing hard things and avoiding the easy things.

The problem with this is that the things you're best at will not feel laborious and difficult. So you'll avoid what you're great at because you believe you should have to "grind" and "hustle" to the bank. This will slow you down.

If we take the things we hate or aren't good at doing and replace ourselves with the right people, guess what happens? Someone else gets the opportunity to perform in their unique genius. This results in three things:

- They're going to do it better than you were doing it (because they like it, and the things we like doing, we do with excellence).
- They're going to do it faster than you were doing it (because there is no mental drag or extra tax on bandwidth. The things you do that you do not enjoy always take longer).
- You (and them) will be happier while doing things that fit inside your lanes.

If you remember, proper scale is when you can fund the growth of a business without robbing the goodwill from tomorrow. You can effectively keep the promises your brand makes to the market. And you can keep your moat intact without over-harvesting your goodwill and reputation with people.

One of the best ways to do that is through hiring and deploying a great team. Let's talk about a few models we use in my company to make hiring great people enjoyable.

T3 Team Matrix

The first framework is called "T3 Teams." There are three levels of a team inside this matrix:

- T3 - Labor
- T2 - Manager
- T1 - Decision Maker

When you hire a T3 team member, as discussed earlier, you're hiring people for the work they will be doing. When you hire a T2 team member, you hire managers who manage the labor from T3 team members and ensure pacing is appropriate for the targets set by the organization.

When you hire a T1 team member, you're hiring replacements or duplicates of yourself. These people can make decisions, create goals, replace team members, and make long-term key decisions for the business's good.

All of these levels are broken apart into their respective departments. Your most traditional departments are marketing, sales, operations, and finance. In most organizations, we put client service or support under operations.

So, with a traditional model, you have three layers of a team and four categories or departments. There are now twelve different boxes we can fill in with people.

	Department 1	Department 2	Department 3	Department 4
T1 DECISION MAKER				
T2 Managerial				
T3 Laborer				

The top box (T1) typically only has room for one person. Underneath that (T2) can have two or three, depending on the organization's size. And underneath that (T3), you can have as many as you need.

Think about it this way, let's take the sales department.

- T1: Sales Director
- T2: Account Executive (Closer) Manager and Sales Development Rep (Setter) Manager
- T3: AEs (Closer) and SDRs (Setter); as many as needed

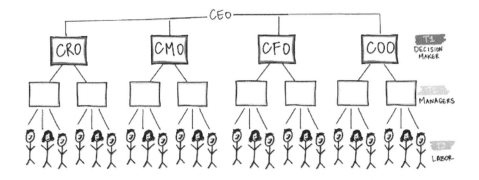

If an organization gets even bigger, you can move the sales director to a C-Suite, and they would likely occupy a Chief Sales Officer or a Chief Revenue Officer role. Be careful with C-Suite titles because you don't want to over-promise as you scale through the different levels of a business.

If your consulting business is under $5M annually in revenue, you won't have many T1 staff members. If you do, they might not be the quality you believe them to be. It's unlikely that a true roster of T1 staff members will allow a business to stay underneath $5M per year.

A common mistake clients make when we begin working together is calling someone a T1 staff member who is really a T2 staff member. If someone cannot rival or exceed you in decision-making, they are not a T1. If you have a T1 that you constantly have to correct or show how to think or make decisions for, they are a T2 member in a T1 seat. You'll have to bump them down at some point or slow the scale of the business down.

The fastest way to jump levels quickly is to hire other T1 players from other organizations. They bring their education and experience when they come in, and the business typically moves forward because of it.

On this note, I want to break down three key metrics to rate your hiring scorecards. This is relevant if you're examining a new hire or considering replacing an in-house team member.

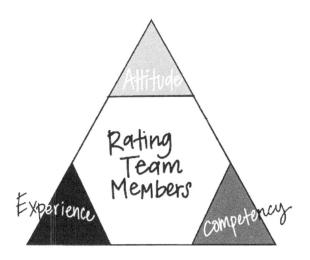

Rating Team Members

We use three key metrics when hiring or rating a candidate's "likelihood" of success. Here they are:

1. Attitude
2. Competency
3. Experience

Attitude is the most important. We don't hire talented people with bad attitudes. We have a list of values and standards for our team, and if you're not a culture fit, you don't belong on the team.

Attitude breaks apart into three areas:

- Positivity
- Coachability
- Communication

Are they positive or negative?

Do they take coaching and criticism well?

Do they communicate with us, or do they hide?

Competency is the second, and this is the skill set we're looking for them to perform at. I'd rather pay in compensation than in competency. What that means is many people will try to save some money, at the expense of excellence. You will pay more for competent people, but it will always be a profitable trade in the end.

Experience answers the question, "Have they done what I'm hiring them to do before?"

You can hire a great player with experience at one level, but they don't have the experience at the level you want them to take the business to. This is okay, but it means you'll have a bit of extra time teaching and guiding them toward your outcomes. A low-competency person will cost you money. A low-experienced person will cost you time.

Compensation

How you pay people is important. There are usually three kinds of compensation:

- Base
- Variable
- Bonuses

My compensation packages typically range from quarterly bonuses to 3-year bonuses. We help customize these with clients. It sounds complicated, but it's essential.

Our 3-year bonuses hold everything to a standard of accountability because they're long-term. A common term in finance is "return on invested capital" (ROIC). If you don't invest, you can't create a return. Perhaps no capital investment will ever be as significant as the payroll and compensation you pay your people.

Revenue Per Head (RPH)

The next framework is your "revenue per head." This was based on a study I read going through Google's financials and seeing how they compensated their leaders. We'll cover this briefly.

Revenue / Team size = RPH
$4,500,500 / 15 = $300,033

The key performance indicator for RPH is $400,000 per year per employee. This comes from a wide-ranging data set of over 2,000 consulting clients I've worked with since 2015. I've worked with some of the best and most profitable companies in the consulting world, and I can tell you that a $400k RPH is hard to do, but it's definitely doable.

It doesn't mean your business is bad or underperforming if you're underneath this. Instead, it indicates that your team is not a 10/10 on the key metrics above or that you have too many players in the business who are not pulling their weight.

We sometimes decide to forgo this metric and keep a lower RPH because we're strategically preparing for scale. For instance, at the time I'm writing this, my RPH for wealthyconsultant.com is $386,000. I am underneath my RPH frameworks, but we are staffed for a bit of scale that we haven't experienced yet. If you're reinvesting back into the business, sometimes your RPH will drop beneath $400k, and that's fine if it's strategic.

This metric is designed to tell you when two things are happening in your business:

- You have too many staff.
- You have unqualified staff.

Both will result in your RPH dropping below the allowable threshold of $400k.

Example: A Business with
Revenue of $4,500,500

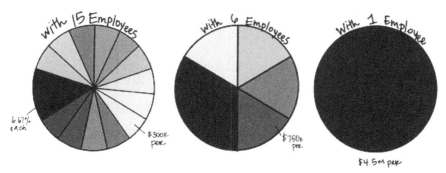

When you put the right person in the proper role, you will notice something happening — they will create their own yields and pay for themselves. A great team is not an expense; it is an investment. Your job is to make the right investments. This framework will help you do that.

You cannot scale if your team is unworthy of scale. This is why you must reserve all your team spots for A players. Notice I did not say reserve your "T1" spots; I said all of your spots. This includes T1, T2, and T3. Today, even my front-level labor is A+ talent.

We have an incredible staff. If you ever want to see what a great team looks like, you can buy more stuff from me and interact with more people. You get access to my leadership team as a high-level client. Any department at any level of labor inside any of my organizations is at your disposal.

Clients get access to them so they can ask questions, get feedback, and design their businesses. Imagine the power of talking to my C-Suite, my marketing directors, my sales leaders, and operational executives.

Sometimes the value people extract from being a client comes more from my team than me!

Addendum and Update (Advanced Nuance)

As a quick aside, I must add an addendum to this chapter.

Business is a collection of people and systems. If those people and systems deliver value to the marketplace, the business will continue to operate. If it's delivering value to the marketplace in a unique way that's hard to find in other places, then the business will naturally take market share. So, it's the job of the team to ensure that value is being distributed to the market in unique ways that are new and interesting. You create a "moat" when that value is delivered in a way that's difficult to rival.

You've probably often heard this quote, "Right people, right seats." This means you have the right person; that's half the battle. You must also put the right person in the right seat or position. The talent has to be situated in the seat that matches their talents, competencies, and experiences. You cannot take a great sales leader and put them over finance. They will fail. You can't take someone great at finance and move them to the head of sales. This seems obvious, but we'll often take a T3 player, promote them to a T2 leadership role, and expect them to excel. Usually, they don't.

The right player in the wrong seat will struggle. There's a third variable that I've recently discovered, and that's the right version. Here's the formula:

Right Person + Right Seat + Right Version = Success

Human beings are not static; we are ever-evolving. Our personalities ebb and flow. It's my experience that certain seasons bring out the best in people, and it's our job as leaders to help regulate the irregularities and create baselines for people. We can do this through culture.

A good culture decreases organizational variability by consistently bringing a person's best version to the surface. It's your job to ensure people are pulled forward by a healthy vision and committed long-term to the organizational mission. This "pull" creates enthusiasm.

At one point, one of my sales teams for a training company long ago, was talented but not producing like they could have. I knew they were capable of more. The problem was a low level of energy & enthusiasm, which was trickling into their work ethic. It wasn't good — so I decided to start re-designing the culture. I created bonuses, trips, awards, and recognition for people who were doing an exceptional job. Do you know what happened? People began to show up early and stay late. They were excited again. The same players, in the same seats, but different versions showed up.

Culture encompasses three key areas:

1. What we believe.
2. Why we believe it.
3. How strongly we believe it.

Even if you get the right T1, T2, and T3, it will always be your job to ensure people believe the right things for the right reasons. Then, you can use compensation, meetings, and planning to strengthen those core beliefs. The stronger the beliefs, the more enthusiastic people will be (assuming they fit your organizational mission). A good culture should remove people who don't stand for what you believe as an organization.

You want your culture to turn your organization into a "self-cleaning" system. It is self-regulating, self-propelling, and to be honest, when you get your culture dialed in, it's almost like magic in that it will heal itself. It's like the body. If there's a viral infection or something that does not fit the standards, it will be secluded, pushed out, or rejected. This is what happens when you have a great culture.

It's a common trap to think that a good culture is always welcoming and happy and everyone is always friendly. That's an incorrect assumption. A great culture will be abrasive to the wrong culture fit. Good cultures do not accept everybody. Good cultures do not bend their standards for people who aren't hell-bent on achieving the collective mission. Good cultures always reflect nature: the fittest survive, and if you are not fit, you cannot stay.

A great culture rewards the team's best players and punishes the team's weak ones. This is when your business becomes scalable because it doesn't necessitate constant "top-down" management or accountability; instead, it creates "bottom-up" accountability from the front lines to the top.

If you want an inside look at how I cultivate and manage teams in every business that I run, I have a special free tool you can access right now at wealthyconsultant.com/team.

CHAPTER 5

Scaling Acquisition

"You have to either (a) find a way to fit your message into that slice of attention, or (b) expand the amount of attention they're willing to give you." - Aaron Ross

When we talk about acquisition, we're talking about turning attention into followers, leads, subscribers, and customers. We've talked about attention in this book, but we are about to go deeper.

They say there's no such thing as "bad attention," but that's probably not true. I believe that attention is nothing more than directed energy. If you've ever stayed up late at night watching YouTube videos - you know the algorithm is a pro at keeping you hooked. I'll start by watching an interview of a famous investor or a popular author, and before I know it, I'm glued to the screen watching alligators eat each other, and I'm like, "How did this even happen?"

They're hacking my attention using dopamine and misusing the power of attention. It doesn't make me want to buy anything from the video; I'm not motivated to move or implement any of the material I'm consuming; it's a waste of time.

Bad attention doesn't inspire action. It simply wastes time.

All attention has an energy signature, so we want to attach a positive (action-oriented) energy signature to the attention we're receiving. There are a few different attention platforms, and we'll use all of them before the business is fully scaled up.

Nothing grows without attention. It's impossible to grow something without acquiring the attention and intention of the market you're selling to. You've never heard of a successful business that did not profitably secure the attention of its market. You can't have a customer without first having their attention.

Earlier, we talked about the differences between getting attention and retaining attention. A basic refresher for you:

- You train people to perform a skill.
- Customers give you money, and you give them value.
- If you give them more value than they paid for, they feel good about it.
- If they feel good about it, they're likely to give you more money in the future.
- You repeat this cycle, and you have a book of business.

But beware: as soon as they give you money, and you don't give them more value in return for their money, they will stop giving you money. I have a problem with everything being free because it does not mirror nature or how the world generally works.

People are used to paying for things that they care about. All things are a trade-off.

Imagine going to Chick-fil-A and saying, "Please give me value first. I don't have money, but I need a chicken sandwich." Or going into Starbucks, walking up to the barista, and saying, "Hello, I don't have money today, but I need a coffee, please. If I like it, I'll pay you." It doesn't work that way.

We only give free content to the marketplace because we will sell them something later. Attention without the intention to sell them something is bad attention. It is worthless, unprofitable, and a waste of time.

Look at Jimmy (Mr. Beast) for a minute. He's published *YouTube* videos and secured the attention of hundreds of millions of people. Then he starts a candy company, and what does he do? Sell them candy. The attention is taken, stewarded well, then converted into something tangible by selling them something.

We want to use the attention platforms I'm about to break down to do the same thing, essentially arbitrating something "invisible" into something "tangible." This chapter gets tactical, and over the next several chapters, we're going to stay in the tactical lane so you can implement.

There are three sections we will cover that form a flywheel of sorts to grow your company's safety: attention, demonstration, and monetization.

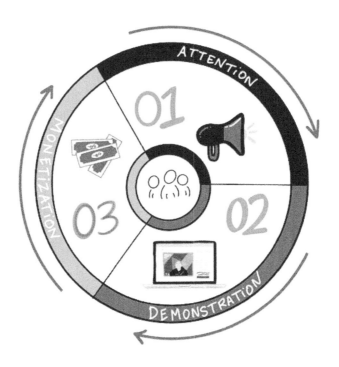

Four Platforms for Getting Attention

Back in the first chapter of this book, I used the term "concentration risk." Concentration risk is actually a banking term that has made its way into the business sector. It describes the level of mounting instability that results from lack of diversity in a banking institution's portfolio. Let's apply this to consulting businesses for a moment. Attention is your currency. The means by which you acquire that attention are your "portfolio." If you become too reliant on any one means of acquisition, your concentration risk increases, and it becomes more and more difficult to pivot fast enough into other platforms. I built this model to alleviate that risk, add diversity, and allow my businesses to stay resilient and durable.

We can use four main models, each of which costs you something. Some cost money and others cost time.

Number 1 — Paid Media

Paid media is the easiest and, in most cases, the fastest. If you're looking to start fast and scale big quickly, you must have paid media in the mix. If we aligned the four types of media acquisition on a graph, from left to right, paid media would be on the left because it's fast and easy. You pay to play.

Remember, we're only talking about attention and acquisition here. Simply learning how to run ads will not create scalability. It largely depends on what you send people to *after* the ad that creates scale. That's covered in the next chapter.

Paid media is viable and needed for every company I own and operate, but we typically "cap" paid media to 50% of attributable revenue. If I generate $20 million annually in revenues, I don't want more than $10 million of it to be tied to paid media. If you're reading this and you're a sophisticated marketer, you might wonder, *How do you define attribution?* After all, if someone comes from an ad, but they don't buy anything for two years, is the sale still attributed to paid media? The answer is no because, at that point, paid media is not responsible for the sale. If someone is on our list or has been consuming our content for the past 120 days, they are now a product of the holistic organization, not just the paid media.

The risks are numerous with paid media. A platform can change an algorithm, and you're out of business. They can mess with your tracking like Apple did with Facebook, and you are blind. Supply chain issues can hurt you if you depend entirely on paid media. If you're selling a product that costs $10 to make and sells for $20, you're great. But if that product costs $20 to make and you have advertising costs, a $20 is now underwater and negative.

If a business is 100% driven by paid media, that is problematic, and you should never scale that way. It isn't safe. Just because people do it doesn't mean it's a great idea.

Number 2 — Organic Media

Organic media can use the same "platforms," but how you access the audience is different. With paid media, you're buying an ad that is put in front of the consumer. With organic media, they are coming to you to look at your content.

Organic takes a long time but is worth the effort. Organic media creates dedicated, long-term followers. The payment medium for building on paid media is currency or money. The payment medium for building on organic media is your time and consistency. Most people are consistent for about two weeks before moving on to other shiny objects.

I've been publishing organic content consistently for over eight years, and it's paid off many times over.

You can also create organic media following through content publications on news outlets and press releases. These forms of media push people to your organic profiles, and people can subscribe to your *YouTube, Twitter, LinkedIn, Facebook, Instagram*, etc. They can sign up for email newsletters and text broadcast lists if they have links inside those platforms. These are phenomenal ways to create long-term relationships with your audience.

I have a strong preference for organic media because it leads with value. Organic media's "conversion" point is to get the relationship, not the transaction. Because of this, your organic media typically produces a higher yield even though it's slower to scale. Over time, it doesn't matter. Once the snowball of organic media is rolling, the only way to stop it is to stop publishing — and even then, it will take a while to stop.

Number 3 — Partnerships

Next up, we have partnerships.

I put JVs, affiliates, and paid shoutouts underneath partnerships. If you've ever been reading an email newsletter or listening to a podcast and heard the phrase, "This show is sponsored by…"

You're hearing a partnership in action.

Partnerships are typically paid engagements that allow you to access someone else's organic or paid media. These are excellent because you're monetizing off the trust of someone else's platform. When my wife and I moved to Nashville, she had to rebuild her hair salon. One of the things we started working on was this simple question: How do we find people who need a new stylist?

We lived in an apartment then and thought, *Plenty of people are moving into our apartments because they just moved here.* They probably don't have a hairstylist if they just moved here. So, we put together a bundle for the apartment to offer "welcome gifts." A free cut and color consult, just for being in the area. If you want to know a crazy industry to get into — it's women's hair.

My wife has people fly to Tennessee from Missouri and Texas to get cut and colored. It's recession-proof as well. I never understood how much money people spent on their hair until I married my wife. A few clients from that campaign still come in every month to get their hair done all these years later.

Referrals, specifically paid referrals, would be another source of partnerships. You're paying someone for the people they bring to you. Anytime you access somebody else's network or reputation, you use partnerships.

Number 4 — Outbound

Outbound is the hardest, but in some regards, it's also the safest. It's safe because it depends almost entirely on human labor. There's not a lot that can interfere with a good outbound process.

When I say outbound, I mean literally "cold" outreach. A lot of companies generate leads and phone numbers, then call them. That's not exactly "outbound." It's still dialing a phone number that was sent to you.

One of my first sales leaders sold door to door, giving out pamphlets to people needing internet services. This is outbound. It is hard, grueling work, but the scalability is linear and predictable. If Facebook shuts down, so what? Suppose the internet goes away; oh well. Human beings still live in houses with phone numbers, and you can still get ahold of them the old-fashioned way. If they don't have phone numbers, you can send them mail. If they can't get mail, you can physically knock on their door.

Attention vs. Transaction

The world works off of value and capital exchange. When someone gives you value, you give them capital. This works both ways. Attention is a form of capital that must be reciprocated with value.

Whether that value comes first (before capital exchange) or second (after capital exchange) depends on your model. In most cases, if you're utilizing the internet, your value precedes the exchange of capital; in this case, "attention" is the capital.

All four of these attention platforms create surpluses of attention. Most people start with paid because it's easy, but if you're going to scale, you must begin working on the others before you have to.

CHAPTER 6

Demonstration

"Nearly every client I've ever worked with was only displaying a third of the proof they actually possessed." - Dan Kennedy

Demonstration is one of the most important elements in making your business work at scale. We've talked about attention. We've talked about your team. We've discussed the different types of leverage and how to create multipliers in your "machine." Now we need to talk about conversion.

An interesting thing happens as you grow — you run out of people who know you. This is why you have different tiers of the market:

- Cold: never heard of you before.
- Warm: know who you are but aren't committed yet.
- Hot: know you, like you, trust you.

Most businesses start by converting the "hot market" into customers or clients. Then they use marketing materials to work on their warm market. Your marketing doesn't have to be that good to convert a warm market because they're already paying attention. When looking to grow or scale quickly, you must be great at turning "cold" into "warm."

Cold market does not trust you. How would they? They're bombarded with ads, and even if they decide to give you their information, they won't be willing to give you money unless you have enough proof or certainty to make it worth the risk. The more expensive your materials are, the warmer someone will need to be to buy from you.

There's a common idea in the marketplace today that you should be able to turn the cold market into paying clients quickly as long as your marketing is great. This is stupid.

I've heard folks stand on stage and preach things like, "Why sell something cheap when you can sell something expensive, and it's just as hard to sell something expensive as it is to sell something cheap?" This is stupid.

You likely put more thought and research into buying a vehicle or a house than buying this book. Why? Because the book is cheap, the house is not. It is a lot easier to sell something cheap. The only real way to "skip" this process is by selling something to *extremely* high-pain markets. If you're a surgeon and the patient has 4 days to live, then they will go off a recommendation and move quickly. For most of us, that's not the situation — nor do we want it to be.

Expediency Kills Scale

We don't want to do something as "quickly" as possible. We want to do it as "certainly" as possible. I am swapping out "speed" for "predictability" here.

I don't like systems that chase expediency at the expense of certainty. Something that hits 50/50 is less valuable than something that hits 80/20 or 90/10. So, with this game of turning "strangers" into "clients," I'm comfortable letting it take some time. To do this effectively, we use a method called "demonstration." A good demonstration asset shows people that you are legitimate, can be trusted, and are a good long-term solution for what they're trying to fix.

It can be effective to view your different demonstration assets in a range from left to right. On the left side, we have things that work quickly but less consistently. On the right, we have things that work slowly and methodically, and they work with devastating effectiveness.

You want to have at least three of these before scaling something. Before we tackle these assets, let's discuss something important. We aren't looking for just any kind of lead, we want the right leads. Here's how to make sure you're generating the type of quality you need for your demonstration to be effective.

Top of Funnel to Bottom of Funnel

This line from left to right can also be turned into a "grid" that works from top to bottom. This goes back to the definition of cold, warm, and hot, which we discussed earlier, and we can overlay this understanding of markets into our demonstration assets.

Your "top of funnel" will be the broadest range of people. Go ahead and compare/contrast these two types of messages:

- How to build long-term retainer patients for small dental practices?
- How to get patients for your practice?

One is wide; one is narrow. The top is narrow and specific, while the bottom is broad and "untargeted." Old-school marketers will tell you to use specific "niche" targeting, but a lot of this methodology is outdated. The world has changed, and you must change with it. In order to scale, you must use both wide and narrow. Said another way, it's not about "choosing" one or the other, it's about using both, but in different places.

Your "top of funnel" is about attracting people to the opportunity you're providing or the problem you're solving. This is for the cold market. Typically, the items you provide as demonstration assets at the top of the funnel will be free. They are PDFs, free trainings, free webinars, blog articles, podcasts, etc.

The middle of the funnel is where it gets a bit narrower and more specific. This is where people turn into a warm market. They're consuming your material, perusing your demonstration assets, and as they do, they build up trust in you and your brand. The "middle-of-funnel" territory is where you start collecting more information. You can then easily go from collecting information to collecting money, all in the middle of your funnel.

Your "bottom of funnel" is for the long-term buyers who are settled on you as a solution provider. This is where the serious money is made, and the real businesses are grown. If you can build a robust bottom of the funnel (a suite of products that people buy, keep buying, and stick around for), then you can spend almost any amount of money to fill up the top of the funnel because you know at some point it's going to convert into profit for you.

I can't stress this enough. We optimize our entire system here for certainty rather than expediency. The name of the long game is "retention," not "acquisition." I'm going deep with you because the demonstration is key to scaling profitably and safely.

MQL, PQL, SQL

You probably haven't heard many of these terms if you're not a full-time marketer, but that's okay. You're becoming a professional today.

At the top of the funnel, you're just attracting and creating leads. Maybe they're good leads; maybe they're not. A good "top of funnel" is about creating lots and lots of leads. Once you get to the middle of the funnel, you start collecting more information, and with this information, we can qualify the leads.

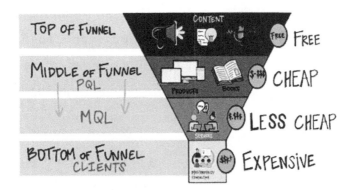

If you've ever heard of "lead scoring," this is a process of scoring the leads and putting parameters around them. Here's an example from one of my businesses:

- A qualified lead makes $500,000 per year.
- An unqualified lead makes less than $100,000 per year.

In this case, the only way to qualify is to know their income; but in other businesses, we have different qualifiers. When a lead is qualified based on the information marketing collects, they're known as a "marketing qualified lead" (MQL). Notice I haven't gotten into intent, not yet. We're still qualifying based on whether they can afford to get help or not.

We qualify leads at scale in two main ways: (a) Need and (b) Time. A *need* qualification answers the fundamental question: Do they even need what my business provides? A *time* qualification answers the next question: Do they have the resources to solve it now, or will they solve it later? Need deals with intent, and time deals with the more normal "constraints" around whether they can actually become a client now or later.

Let's say you have a training company that helps general contractors win more contracts, and you publish a report that says, "Eleven Ways to Get Long-Term Contracts Without Having to Advertise." Many folks will download this, but they're not all going to be qualified. If someone downloads this report and is a general manager at a local zoo, well, they're entirely outside your market. They will not pass the "Need" qualifier because they don't need what your business does for them. They're a lead but not a qualified lead.

Let's say another lead comes in, and they are right in your target market. They are perfect. But upon examination and data provided by the lead, they're so broke they can barely afford to keep the lights on. This lead would qualify on the "Need," but they would not qualify based on "Time." Why? They can't afford to do the requisite work to get the problem fixed right now. You can offer scholarships or discounts, but you cannot charge this lead money because they will not have it. There are many ways to collect data and information from your leads, and we can help you with that; it's part of what we do.

First, we must decide what types of qualifiers we want to optimize for. At the top, we have "leads," and underneath that, we have MQL, which is qualified based on the marketing data we collected. The next level is when someone goes from opting in for information to sending you money for training. This takes them further down, known as a "product qualified lead" (PQL). You can categorically put MQL and PQL on the same level, but a PQL will be more likely to go one step further into the bottom of the funnel.

When Jeff Bezos launched Amazon Prime, he lost money on it for years. He didn't create the subscription to make more profit; he created it to retain more customers. If you're an Amazon Prime subscriber and get free shipping, you're more likely to buy something from Amazon. When you are willing to lose money on the front end because you will retain them on the back end, this is known as a "loss leader." Nothing will be more profitable for you than generating good customers and keeping them forever. You are much more likely to create clients if you turn them into customers first.

The "Holy Grail" of scale is the acquisition of great leads; then sorting those leads into qualified and unqualified (MQL); then turning qualified leads into customers (PQL); then retaining the customers until they turn into clients (bottom of the funnel).

The phrase to remember when you're in this stage is "Serve & Segment."

- Serve them with great content, training & information
- Segment them based on what they engage with or interact with

The goal is to never sell someone something they do not need, but in order to do this, we must have them segmented enough to understand them before selling something.

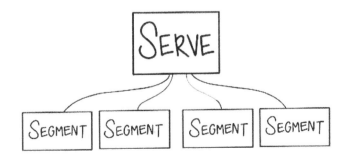

This isn't easy, but it's worth the effort. You can't just sell something, waste the customer's time, and tell them to buy more stuff. At each level, the value must exceed whatever investment they made, whether they paid in time or money. I've never had someone give me money, fail them, and then have them turn around and give me more money. People don't do that.

People only keep buying if they are satisfied and feel that you have fulfilled the promises of the prior product. We can use the example of the book you're reading now. You bought this book. You're in our system somewhere as a PQL because you gave us money. Assuming you are in our market, and you're qualified (both on need and time), it's likely you are pleased with this product and will likely, at some point in the future, give us more money to help you do something in the future. The value of the book dwarfs the money you paid for the book. Guess what? Every product you can buy from us should be the same way. It only makes sense that the more value you get, the further you will want to go.

Eventually, you decide to be "in the room" or working hands, which is a great decision. The advantages and benefits of this decision are wide-ranging: access to our done-for-you teams, our tech setups, our pipelines, and back-end management systems, our account executives, daily consulting and masterminds, communities filled with rock stars and trainers/coaches/consultants who are world-class at what they do, etcetera.

You're literally in the middle of a scalable system right now. That's what we build with clients but for their particular brand and market.

This book is one type of "demonstration asset" we use across our portfolio of companies and clients. We use the demonstration assets to show (aka prove) we know what we are doing.

Six Demonstration Assets

Now that we know the different types of quality for our leads let's talk demonstration. There are six main demonstration assets you should be using in your business as you scale. We'll go in order from "fastest" and "easiest" to the "most certain" but most difficult.

Keep in mind that the more difficult it is to create, the higher the barrier to entry will be. If you have a lot of difficult demonstration assets in the market, you will be harder to compete with. Not all markets are equal. Some are highly competitive, and some are quite open. We can connect later and help you look at the competitive landscape and customize the assets you put to market.

Direct Offers

The first and easiest demonstration asset is the "direct offer."

Direct offers include things that make direct offers, such as webinars, video sales letters, and other sorts of "pitches" that waste no time getting to the offer. Remember that, according to publicly available research, roughly 3-5% of a market is willing to buy quickly. They're in a place of need, have the money to move, and need something to work. Just because you get a direct offer working doesn't mean you should be scaling it.

True scale is when you can create a new market, not find the top 3-5% and convert them. Average acquisition systems "find" clients and customers. Great acquisition systems "create" clients and customers over time.

Communities

Communities are gatherings of people, such as *Facebook* groups, Discord groups, Telegram lists, and even email lists. These work incredibly well if your market tends to make decisions using other people. A community is where you can publish content, handle objections, and show successful examples of your brand.

The beauty of a community is rather than one person seeing it in a vacuum, they're seeing how other people respond to the content in real-time. I used to run a large *Facebook* group filled with entrepreneurs. When someone would be curious about our programs or ask to talk to past clients, we'd say, "Sure, go post in the group and ask for some current or past clients."

This happened just a few weeks ago while I was in the middle of editing this manuscript. I will show you here, so you can see the power of community as a demonstration asset. One of our products for a consulting & training brand is called "LaunchKit." It's for newer experts who want to set up and mobilize a training or consulting company. It's not built for established businesses who are already scaling, it's for people who are looking to get started.

He posted in one of our communities and asked a question about the product. This happened before he made a purchase decision, and current members saw it and added their two cents.

If you have a good product, you can see how this greatly improves your demonstration because it "proves" that you have great expertise and a great product. The downside is that if you don't have a great product, people will post their opinions about that, and you can't remove them. You must be willing to let *all* opinions be shared — so communities only work well if you're committed to your product and are willing to handle both positive and negative feedback.

One of my colleagues selling life insurance puts together a monthly physical get-together. This has turned into a community of like-minded people interested in the same thing: securing long-term insurance as an investment vehicle. Whenever someone has questions, he invites them to the next meet-up, and they get to see the legitimacy of what he does.

Events

An event is a virtual or "in-person" get-together that works to train and educate a group of people all at once. The main difference between a community, and an event, is the start and end date. An event has a definitive "start date" and a definitive "end date." An event is a one-day, two-day, or maybe even three-day offering. A community is an ongoing, never-ending "gathering" that people belong to.

A significant benefit to running an event is you're typically getting people entirely focused for an extended period. The attention is high, and the density of information is high. You can make a pitch at the end if you want to and then merge the benefits of three kinds of attention assets: events, communities, and direct offers.

Products

After events, we have products.

You should have noticed by now that these different categories tend to "layer" together. A product, which creates a PQL (product-qualified lead), is a great form of demonstration. Whenever someone has to pay to access something, they will pay more attention to it.

If an event is a paid event, you're layering four types of demonstration assets together. In most cases, though, when we build products as demonstration assets, we're not referring to events but courses or other pieces of paid material.

Books

Books are one of my favorites because they're hard to do. Anybody can write "a book," just like anybody can create "a course." However, writing a good book is difficult. Many folks say writing a book is easy if you just have the right system, but let me share something with you: they're just marketing to you.

Writing a good book is pretty tough, and if something is hard to do, it will be hard to compete with. Try writing a 100 to 200-page book if you're not an expert at what you're writing about; you can't do it. This is why books are a tremendous form of demonstration. The main difference between a book and a product is that books are widely trusted and globally distributed. I'm talking about books that are published and distributed across major bookstores, physical and digital.

This book is a perfect example. It would have been easier to write the book and put a PDF on the internet, but my goal isn't to create a product. I want a book. You can hold it, highlight, read, and re-read it. Books are the oldest medium of information transfer, outside of oratory and audible learning.

Content

The final piece of demonstration is your content. This is the last and most difficult because it requires the most consistency. To make content productive (and profitable), you must be willing to do it for a long time. I've been publishing content consistently on *Facebook* for almost ten years.

If you find any of my material on *LinkedIn, Twitter, Facebook,* or *YouTube,* you know that a lot of effort goes into producing great content repeatedly. Podcasts fit inside this demonstration asset, and I have (at this point) almost a thousand episodes on my main podcast, "The Good Life w/Taylor Welch." It is hard to fake a thousand episodes. I believe in content so much that I acquired a content agency that publishes content for experts, trainers, and consultants.

All of my content is produced, edited, and syndicated through my content agency.

It might feel overwhelming at first, but you need to start somewhere. You don't have to do all platforms like I do, but pick one and stay with it. Even when nobody is seeing or engaging with it, eventually, you'll have a bed of content, and people will start paying attention.

Demonstration in a Nutshell

The beauty of having a solid system for demonstration is it makes scale "inevitable." You can layer demonstration assets together and link them together. When you view a piece of content, it can link to a direct offer. If your content is great, you can promote an event from your content. At the event, you can give out copies of your book. These things all tie into one another, and before long, if it's set up correctly, you've got a "web" of assets showing the market you know what you're doing and can be trusted. Here's an example of this kind of layering:

- You're reading a book that you paid for
- If you want more content from me, you should go to taylorawelch.com and start looking at my content
- My social platforms are all
  @taylorawelch (Twitter.com/taylorawelch,
  Facebook.com/taylorawelchprofile,
  Instagram.com/taylorawelch, etc.)

Now, hopefully, you will not only have read this book, but you'll start getting practical, applicable content from me on a consistent basis. This content will help you think better, feel better, and make more money.

Because of this book, and maybe the content, you can find information about events & products that I create. And the entire machine "weaves" together.

I like seeing at least a million dollars per year (of revenue, not profit) per demonstration asset. You never want to scale too big from too few assets. I've done that before, and it's risky business. Keep in mind these demonstration assets are categories. If you have a million dollars a year per asset, it stacks up quickly. If you have two books, a few direct offers, an event per quarter, and a couple of communities, you can do the math. Scale can happen, and it can feel effortless.

CHAPTER 7

Monetization Models

"You create money by increasing your value inside yourself...
You then experience money by exchanging the value you have
built in you. Exchange it with others by providing services, goods,
and money to others in exchange for their services, goods,
and money." - David Gikandi

Let's talk about monetization.

Monetization is the process of turning "attention" into revenue. I teach four main models of monetization, which are designed to help you organize resiliency in your business.

No matter what the economy is doing, you will have multiple ways to collect cash to keep the business growing. Suppose you are advertising and paying money to put your ads in front of people. These models will give you peace of mind that no matter what these platforms do, your revenue won't screech to a halt.

Regardless of whether you have one demonstration asset or twenty, monetization models duplicate the amount of revenue you can make, just as demonstration assets duplicate the volume of leads you can attract.

Whenever I go into a new business, either as a partner or a consultant, one of the first few things I'm looking to create is a robust monetization system. Advice like "charge more money" or "raise your prices" is antiquated and outdated. You cannot scale a business safely without creating diversity in how you charge the money. It's not always what you charge; it's how you charge it and when.

Remember in Chapter 5 when we talked about "concentration risk" in your attention acquisition channels? If you're smart, you're already extending that idea outward and applying it to other areas of your business. The riskiest (and least safe) businesses are those that are built on "one." One this, one that; one way to get leads, one way to get clients, one way to collect their money. Your methods of monetization are no different. Diversity is critical to sustaining growth, regardless of external circumstances.

I want to teach you in this chapter the different categorical methods used for monetizing expertise.

The Four Monetization Models

The first model is a product.

Products, in most instances, will cost $100 or less, and they're "go at your own pace" for the consumer. A product must have two delineating factors to be considered a product:

- Automated delivery
- No customization

When someone purchases a book, a course, or a "product" from you, they must receive it automatically. You aren't going to be manually sending this out to people who pay for it. Then, every customer who buys a product receives the same experience of the product. This book is monetized using the product model. It's a book (demonstration) with information (level 1 offer), and it's monetized as a product (swipe a credit card, receive information). You're not getting a private, "custom" version of the book. You are reading these words, and thousands of other people are reading these words. Guess what? The words are all the same!

A product is like that; there's no customization.

One of my targets right now is to sell 10,000 products per month to great customers who get great value out of the material. That's 120,000 products per year, and if we do that, we're well on our way to making a nice positive dent in the world. I'm in a unique market with a unique opportunity. Here's why — everyone I help, by default, helps others. If you're a trainer or a consultant, you are helping other people; that's your job.

If I help you, I'm helping you to help more people. My job is multiplicative and highly leveraged. I love that by reading this book, you will be able to help countless more humans do amazing things they would never have been able to do otherwise. There's something more. If you're selling great products, you're doing the same thing for other people.

One of our clients helps busy entrepreneurs create physical vitality. His process involves them sending in their blood work and getting customized coaching and supplementation that helps them sleep better, lose weight, create more energy, and become superheroes! How cool is that?

The more customers he helps, the more people his customers can interact with. Everything in the consulting, training, service, and coaching world is a multiplier. If you're helping people become better (at almost anything), you're creating a ripple effect.

Products are awesome because they reduce your dependency on people and create free advertising. When people buy a book like this, assuming they like it, they end up talking about it. If you're just getting started, you don't need to start with products — you can skip the food chain a bit for some quick wins. But eventually, you need to have *three* of the models collecting money for you.

The Law of the Mirror

On that note, let me take a brief tangent and share one of the best tools for creating a durable business. It's called the Law of the Mirror.

In 2017, I was on a sales call, and it was anything but ordinary. The reason it was so out of the ordinary is there were four or five other sales reps with me on the call. They were listening in the background, taking notes. This was one of my old teams that I hired and managed. This particular prospect was desperate. His business was flailing, and he'd been trying for two years, unsuccessfully, to fix it. One of his biggest issues was that people would say they wanted to move forward with him (he helped big CRM companies improve their systems and operations) and then back out or delay until they didn't need help anymore.

I explained the process we used, and he was excited. When it came down to the end, when he had the chance to engage my firm and let us help him, he said this, "I like it, and I'm in… I need to take a few days and think about it to make sure it's the right time. Then I'll get back to you."

I said, "You've got to be kidding me!" He was taken aback by this and asked me why I said it. I said, "I think you've just given me my first data point for why your business is struggling."

He said, "What is it?"

I replied, "Well, it's you! People will behave with you exactly how you behave with them and others." The lesson is clear. If you want better clients, be a better client. If you want to get paid on time, you pay on time. If you want people to respect you, start by respecting yourself. The mirror runs our perception of the world, and that perception of the world is predictive. We are the cause, not the effect.

One of the most powerful models I've ever learned is that I create the world by the way I treat the world. This person was gracious enough to pause and respond from a place of contemplation rather than a place of ego. The Bible and countless older texts agree on this: you reap what you sow. I've always made it a habit of mine to sow the types of things I'd like to reap.

I want to help you do that now if you're open to it.

There are many excellent people in the world who are struggling with the components required to build a successful, durable business. They have the tools and experiences but don't have the right recipe. One of the reasons I wrote this book is to break down some of the recipes I have learned so more people can create surplus and security for themselves and the ones they care about.

The Problem

If people don't see or read the book, the book cannot help them. If you have ever published material (books, posts, podcasts, newsletters, etc.), you know how valuable it is to read the reviews and feedback from those who've consumed your work. It is a joy, and there's nothing as motivating. The reviews also help ensure more people see and read the material. The more people who see the book, the more people the book can help.

If you want to execute the Law of the Mirror and sow the things you want to reap, a great (and free) way to do that is by leaving a review for this book. There are people who will see the book because of your review, but just as importantly, the law of the mirror will be activated in your own life. We attract what we put out.

I would love for you to take two minutes tops and leave an honest, unbiased review of this material. If you feel inclined, it will mean the world to me. Here is how to do that:

Go to *Amazon.com* and search for the title of this book. Scroll to the bottom and click "Leave a review." If you're on Kindle, click toward the bottom of your screen and click "Rate this book."

Just state whatever your honest opinion is, and I'm sure it will be helpful.

Now back to the book!

A Caveat: Expensive Products

You're not going to be selling products for $10k or $100k, even though there are technical products that cost that much. Automobiles and houses come to mind, but those are different types of businesses.

Let's address this quickly so we can use the model and think about it correctly. We have a "gross" margin and a "net" margin with all products. Your gross margin is what you have left over after the costs to create the product are paid. With net margin, you have the true bottom line of the business, meaning after all staff, software expenses, building leases, and other fulfillment items are paid.

A house might cost $500,000 to build and sell for $650,000. This is a gross margin of 23%. When you pay team, software, and all other operating costs, you might have a bottom line of $50,000. This is a net margin of 7%. For expensive products, this isn't abnormal. For our model, we're talking about training products, books, courses, recordings, and things of a similar nature. Your gross margin on these products should be 90% or higher.

On a fulfillment scale, it's a zero out of four. There's no fulfillment except for your software delivering the product. Monetizing using products means you're automating everything. Someone sends money, they receive a piece of information in exchange.

Model: PRODUCT
Cost: $100-$1,000
Fulfillment: 0/4

The Second Model is Services

Services break from "education" or training and enter the realm of labor. You're not showing them how to do something or fix an issue; you're fixing it for them.

Many training companies and consulting firms tend to stay out of services, but it's an incredible tool to retain clientele. Resilient firms include some labor as a way to remove obstacles from the client. To identify what services to offer or "bolt-on," you can go through this exercise.

Imagine the client's journey as a line from the left to the right. On the left, there is the start of the client relationship. On the right is "completion." In the middle, there are three or four areas where clients lose their way, slow down, get confused, frustrated, or distracted.

List these areas and circle them. For instance, if you're helping the female entrepreneurial market secure funding for their startup, let's say there are three or four areas where your clients lose some momentum.

One could be the pitch deck. The next could be cold outreach to potential investors. Whatever these areas are, I'm showing you an example. An easy way to add services would be to build a pitch deck for them. You can hire someone cost-effectively and then use proper onboarding and data collection to get the details. You don't even have to charge for this; it can be a part of your consulting offer that you do for them.

This is a fantastic way to not only sign more clients but to keep them because they won't get stuck. They'll move quickly, and when people move quickly through a proven process, they tend to get results quicker and tell more people. The other opportunity you have for services is identifying where people go "next." When they are no longer in need of your consulting or your program, what do they need next?

If you can identify where someone goes, you can build the next thing as a service and keep them longer. We can help you build all of this out; it's something we often do, and it's a terrific tool for building resiliency in down markets.

Model: SERVICE

Cost: $50,000-$1M

Fulfillment: 4/4

A Quick Note About Self-service

This isn't a monetizing model, but it's a nifty trick I want to teach you; an alternative lens to create services is to ask, "What areas do I need the most help with?" For example, as I have trained experts on how to build growth-oriented, resilient businesses, one thing that people always need is paid media. That's a form of attention, so I built a paid media agency with a friend and partner. They run the ads for all of my brands and also for clients.

Another service I needed was social media management. If you follow me on any social media platform, you'll see a consistent stream of content from me and my business. That's because we created an agency specifically to handle this. This is all created and managed professionally by our in-house agency. Then we took that agency and made it available to consulting clients. This is referred to as vertical integration.

Our job is to make our client's businesses more profitable, fun, effective, and durable. Anything you're paying money for, if we can do it, we'll bring it in-house to make it easier and more efficient.

The Third Model — Programs

As an educator, you can transfer your expertise, experience, skills, intelligence, perspectives, or ideas to your clients. You might remember from an earlier chapter that we talked about different levels of productization. You had information, customization, and proximity or access.

This monetization model is where you customize your training or consulting for the client. It gets more specific. A program covers both of the higher-tiered levels of productization — customization and access. Usually, these are separated into different programs that are priced accordingly (proximity is typically more expensive than customization).

We don't recommend selling programs for less than $5,000, and they can get quite expensive. One of my consulting programs is $150,000 for a year of consulting, and people pay it because it works favorably for them. If someone wants to work with me closely to maximize a piece of their business, fix their team or open up new market share opportunities, the $150,000 is cheap compared to the profit potential created.

If you are struggling to sell something for $5,000 or more, you need a better offer or lens through which to view your offer. I will end up helping you with both, depending on how much time we have. Another important note to make with this model is your pricing model. Price is one thing. The pricing model is another.

Let's use the example of the 1:1 consulting retainer. Yes, $150,000 is expensive compared to the cost of a book, but compared to the upside, it isn't that much. What makes it more palatable is the pricing model. It isn't collected all up front, and part of it is tied to revenue creation to be read literally; I'm creating the extra revenue to pay myself, not adding it as a fixed line item in the business.

Some of these clients turn into equity partners, and we build for the long term. Then it becomes even more palatable because I'm acting as an owner. If the business doesn't perform, I don't get paid. If the business does perform, that $150,000 "expense" turns into several million dollars of enterprise equity value for the client. It's important to note that the monetization model changes when I convert a client from a program to a partner. We'll get to that a little bit later on in this chapter.

So, programs can start at $5,000 and work up to hundreds of thousands, potentially millions of dollars. I was in California with a friend who charges $500,000 yearly to meet with him each month. He has ten clients paying him over $40,000 per month, and it's worth it to them because they're receiving more value in return than what they're paying. Some people have so much money they don't know what to do. They're worried that they'll lose it or that they're losing their family. Whatever the problem is, money is not one of them.

You will need to learn to cater to people who have the means to pay you what you want to earn. As long as the value you deliver exceeds the money they're paying, you will have no problem collecting it.

That's an important note to remember as we talk about monetization. Whatever someone pays you in currency, you must repay them more in the currency of value, transformation, security, protection, enhanced results, etcetera. And by the way, we have many programs that are not $150,000 or $500,000. I merely use these as examples to show you what is possible.

Model: PROGRAM
Cost: $5,000-100,000
Fulfillment: 2/4

The Fourth is Partnership

Earlier when I mentioned I take my 1:1 clients and turn them into partners, what is happening is we're jumping into a new monetization model. They might start as a fee-based client, in a program, and move into a partnership client.

Partnership is not reserved for equity partners, though. You can monetize your leads and clients through joint ventures (JV), affiliates, and white labels. One of our products is productivity training. When they buy the product, they unlock a video course, several templates for organizing projects and tasks, and a handful of bonuses. (If you want to check out this product, go to wealthyconsultant.com/productivity). Inside the course is a coupon code for a digital tablet we use in-house. It's an amazing product we highly recommend, so we have no problem recommending and discounting it to our customers. The thing is, we don't build or sell this product. It's a different brand. They gave us a referral partnership so that we could sell their products as an affiliate.

This adds thousands of dollars of partnership income to our monthly books, and we incur zero fulfillment costs; our gross margin is 100%, and all customer support is run through the other company. A friend of mine that I work out with told me this morning that they're paying a $10,000 referral fee for one of their services! They run done-for-you sales team management and training. I said, "$10,000? That's a lot of cash!" He's paying it all day because the clients pay him $50,000. The $10,000 is an acquisition cost to him, but it's partnership revenue for someone else.

Model: PARTNERSHIP
Cost: Infinite
Fulfillment: 1/4

Merging Monetization Models

You can (and should) have multiple monetization models working in unison inside of your business.

Never again will I be in a position where one type of monetization goes down, and I don't have others that could easily replace it. Now you don't need to be either. If you study the biggest companies of all time, most have many different forms of monetization. The longest-lasting training companies utilize all four.

CHAPTER 8

Scaling Fulfillment

"Fulfillment means that the individual has generally fulfilled the basic tasks of a given stage or wave." - Ken Wilber

I'll never forget the first season I experienced true scale. The largest number of clients I'd ever taken was between 12 and 13. I had a small one-person agency and had been writing marketing materials for some impressive businesses.

I started consulting by accident. People got to know me from my work and wanted to know what I was doing to stay booked with clients. One time I turned in a project and marked it as completed. The client received it, loved it, and referred me to someone he knew. The problem was I already had another client I was putting together work for. Instead of telling the referral "No," I told him a price he would never pay. The price was more than double anything I'd charged before. He said, "I'll pay it."

I didn't know what to do, so I explained I already had a client before him. He would have to wait to get started. He said, "Okay, I will wait."

Stumped again, I said, "Well, you will have to pay now, and then we can get started in a month," thinking there was no way he would pay an entire month before the start date.

He said, "Okay do you have a contract, and how do you prefer payment?"

I tried hard to kill that deal. I was busy and didn't need the money. I've heard plenty of people say, "I don't need the money," but they're just posturing for more money. I was legitimately in a season where I did not know what I was doing but was so busy I didn't want the work. This person, though, had seen my previous writing and didn't care how long it took. The secret strategy here was not takeaway selling. It was not my salesmanship (clearly). The driver of my behavior was my work. The legitimacy of my work was the driving factor.

So, this is how my waiting list started; someone wanted to pay and wait. Then it happened again and again. Before long, I had a six-month waiting list. People would ask if they could hire me, and I'd say, "Yes, in six months," and then they started talking. I remember getting random messages from people on social media that sounded like this, "Hey Taylor, nice to meet. I wanted to talk to you about your waiting list and how you built it."

I had no idea who these people were, but I thought it would be worth talking about. So that's what I started doing.

The Journey and the Bottleneck

When I started talking about it, all of a sudden, the questions changed from "How did you do that?" to "How do I do it?" That was my cue to start charging, so I went from "service" business to "consulting." The first client paid me $2,000 monthly and stopped paying after the second month. Why? He got what he needed, built a waiting list, and said, "Thanks, bye!" I hadn't learned the retention and long-term fundamentals at this point. I just knew how to create waiting lists and get clients.

Enough clients were lining up to learn from me that I thought, *Why am I doing services for people? I should teach them instead.* My first consultancy was born. It grew. It grew big. I turned my consulting into a proper product. Today, this is a standard in our organization and for all of our clients. We build consulting firms with durability in mind. However, back then, it was like the Wild West. I was selling customized advisory services with some course material; that was my program. Things started growing quickly. My clients received tremendous results, and they talked. Word of mouth was positive, and thus it grew even faster.

This was my first experience growing something or scaling something quickly.

My dad always said, "Problems are the tuition you pay for the lessons you receive." This was a long time ago, my "program" was hosted in a Dropbox folder online and nobody knew who I was, but the lessons will never be forgotten. It was a season of tuition for me. Sort of like a college degree, but a thousand times more valuable (and expensive).

Two Ideals

The model I have developed for scaling fulfillment revolved around two principal ideals:

1. It must be great for the team.
2. It must be great for the clients.

The reason I teach frameworks is they layer together and protect you from unintended consequences. Frameworks also allow you to hit multiple priorities at once – which is difficult to do if you're making every decision in "real time" based on gut. You can safely build the next level if you get the foundations right. If you get that second level right, you can safely build the third level. If you mess up the second level, everything you build on top of it will break. It's important to create what I call cumulative infrastructure.

Rails for the System to Run On

A couple of months ago, a client asked me how to handle more clients. He knows my philosophy and correctly chose to prioritize reputation over raw speed. He is also a genius. When building great business systems for personal training companies, he's one of the best in the world. The more clients his business onboarded, the harder it was to protect the client experience.

I asked him some questions and discovered the problem. He was driven by intellect and intuition and hadn't done the difficult work of putting his intuition into models and frameworks. I spent a lot of time when I started my last business creating boundaries around my thinking, and, as you can see, a lot of my expertise has been appropriately placed into these models that help you run your business no matter the industry you serve.

This allows you to duplicate not what you do but what you know. Your team begins working off of centralized and cohesive "ideas" implemented and executed repeatedly. It takes a decent amount of work to ensure the model is correct, but once it's validated, it scales quickly.

One of our most important frameworks is the "3 Rails" of fulfillment. These rails provide a solid track for your fulfillment systems to run on. The only possible way to scale your fulfillment is by using some variation of these three rails.

Rail 1: Curriculum

When you enroll in a program at Stanford or Harvard, or the University of Alabama, you pick a degree based on the outcome you're trying to achieve. Then, you go through a list of classes designed to earn that degree. You buy the textbooks and start attending lectures. The lectures are not random but based on the textbook and the professor's unique ability to transfer the information.

The only way for the class to be effective is by using this curriculum. Can you imagine if every new student went through whatever they felt like asking for that day in class? Or if two semesters taught drastically different things based on the professor's mood? No! This would not work.

Curriculum creates "predictability" and "repeatability," so when you take the class, you learn the materials needed to earn the degree. That's what the curriculum is for. Your curriculum is a regulator of the material taught and learned. I figured this out early because people kept asking the same questions repeatedly. To be transparent, I stumbled upon the psychology of this first rail because of sheer laziness. I was tired of repeatedly answering the same thing, so I started writing and recording a curriculum that answered the questions before they were asked.

You should start looking at the things you will need to explain again and again instead of talking about them again and again. Put it into a curriculum so it's taught in advance. Anything that is repeated should be recorded. When you get a great curriculum in place, not only do your client results improve, but the amount of support and calls needed are drastically reduced.

A great curriculum creates an "algorithm" of sorts that guides the nature and certainty of results. Take my recent company, the Wealthy Consultant, and you'll find different tracks of content inside that people choose to go through. There are playbooks and unique implementation days. Think of these as "electives" at the collegiate level. They are topical and provide utility in specific lanes or areas.

These predefined bits of information, organized appropriately into specific applications, form your curriculum. The only way you can scale a fulfillment team or process is by having a repeatable curriculum that people go through instead of showing up and asking all of their questions to you personally.

Rail 2: Community

Most skill sets require the mind. It isn't always intellectual, either. You can take a smart person who believes they are worthless, and they'll lose to a dumb person who believes they deserve to succeed. This is one of the more confounding mysteries in success literature: what you believe is more powerful than what you do.

I noticed that specific trainers or consultants would receive the same information. One would win, and one would not. One of the differences (after examining thousands of them) was their state of mind and their beliefs about themselves. I dealt with this volatility by creating communities that people could join. The curriculum works to regulate the dispensing of information. The community works to regulate the belief systems inside your client roster.

You have likely experienced this phenomenon. Your environment drives your feelings and, thus, your drive and determination. You'll be more motivated to push yourself physically if you're at a gym surrounded by a bunch of physically fit athletes than you'd be at your home alone with a dumbbell. You will be more motivated to build a great business if you're surrounded by other people building great businesses. Struggling together, creating together, learning together.

This rail of community forms the second piece to scale something with excellence, even when scaling fast and big. When I had my first child, it was tremendously helpful for my wife and me to have friends who already had children. When we had questions, we asked them. If you're writing a book, it's great to have friends and acquaintances who have written books because you can talk to them when you're stuck. This is no different than finding a great business community, especially if you're one of the only ones you know who is building a business. It can be lonely, and trust me when I say this: When you find your people, it makes all the difference.

Notice how the community is a support system in and of itself. It can help you stay motivated, inspired, and fired up long after the "honeymoon phase" of starting a new program or hiring a new mentor wears off. I meet with a group of business owners once or twice a year to discuss ideas. One of them runs the largest SaaS training company online. One of them teaches men how to be great husbands and great leaders at home. Another is a mental programmer who has worked with the heads of state of several governments. He is a genius! There are several of us, and we connect, talk about business, and share ideas. I'm also in the coolest group of entrepreneurs and consultants I've ever participated in, but I put it together myself. People say to me all the time, "It's great to be in your mastermind," and I'm quick to correct the record. It's our mastermind. I enjoy getting together with our clients and community as much as they do.

There is no substitute for a good community; it will help you take care of clients at scale. You can engineer a community to help build the beliefs and the energy that people will need to get the job done and win. It takes some time and strategic forethought.

Rail 3: Coaching/Customization

People will always need a way to customize their applications. For example, we were at an event in my hometown here in Nashville. One of our clients, who has been with us for a long time, a wonderful client, helps female entrepreneurs grow their companies. They needed some support with one of their tech stacks because they spend a lot of money on ads and needed ways to track it.

Their CRM tracked the leads but wasn't set up to track them at scale. My team has spent tens of millions of dollars in advertising, so we place a massive amount of importance on our tracking setup. Data is the lifeblood of marketing, and the accuracy of that data is what keeps you from wasting money. Anyways, she talked to me and my head of marketing and showed us how their CRM wasn't tracking MQLs properly. You remember MQLs from an earlier chapter. My marketing leader went into their system, fixed it, and showed them why it wasn't working. This is only possible when you have an arm of the fulfillment machine focused on customization. They told us they'd paid someone $70,000 to build their CRM and were getting ready to pay another $50,000 to bring someone on and build it out further. We probably saved them $50,000 in hard costs and millions in opportunity costs from being unable to track their ads.

This is an example of a client who most likely didn't go through the entire curriculum because they're doing 8-figures a year and don't need to go through content when they're already strapped for time. What they did do, was ask a question, get hands-on support, and find a customized solution to their problem.

Machine is 24/7

When you have a system like this configured for your market, you can enroll clients at any time, be it day or night. You will automate some of the fulfillment and leverage the rest around a predetermined set of rules and principles that always work.

A university can enroll hundreds, or even thousands, of students and care for each of them. That's because they have a system in place designed to handle it. One of the worst mistakes you can make is taking on more clientele than you can effectively fulfill. This hurts your reputation, and that takes time to recover from. The machine is designed to help clientele sort and segment themselves and connect them with the information or tactical skill set they need to reach their destination.

You don't enroll in Stanford, then show up and ask to talk to the Dean each day about your random questions. That's not how it works. You enroll in your classes, show up, do the work, and get the customization available from the professor doing the lectures. Similarly, we have subject matter experts that can aid on virtually any topic that pertains to business. This is another massive bonus for communities regarding fulfillment: It gets more valuable as the community grows. This is known as the "network effect." Each new client who joins the community (provided you are enrolling the right people) is an expert in what they do and enriches the other members simply by engaging in what you've built.

We're modeling this in many different industries and organizations. There are particulars and specifics that we don't have time to cover in this book, but I want to show you categorically that there are three main areas you need to scale fulfillment:

- Curriculum
- Community
- Coaching / Customization

Let's take the time to go deeper into the third category, customization. I'm going to take the time and break this down because I want you to be able to build it on your own if that's what you'd like to do.

Fractionalizing Customization

If you break down customization, you get into what is commonly called "support." There are sub-segments in all three rails that we get into with clients, but customization and support are the most important, so we'll cover that here.

Albert Einstein once said, "Make everything as simple as possible, but no simpler." What I'm trying to convey to you is the simplicity of a well-constructed system without stripping away its robustness. By necessity, a great framework and model will become more complex the deeper you dive into it. This is because it must remain agile as the world moves.

In its simplest form, a vehicle is an engine with some wheels on it. That's quite simple; you must get into the pieces and parts to truly understand it. Each piece and part must be hooked up correctly, and if you hook it into the wrong place, it will not work. This system is no different.

I'll end this chapter with the four categories we use for personalized coaching and customization. While we don't have time to explain it all in detail, this will give you some ideas as to how *we* do it, and if you'd like customized feedback, I'm happy to help.

Classroom

These are calls and conversations that have more than one person. Sometimes they have subject matter experts and go deep on a specific topic. Sometimes they're with a professor, coach, or team member whose job is doing the work they're training on.

Implementation Day

These are typically longer, 3 to 5-hour days that go through a specific topic. They include what, how, who, and when. For example, we've had multiple implementation days around sales, sales teams, customer acquisition, finance and forecasting, and most other segments of running and growing a healthy consulting or training company.

Events

We use events to merge implementation days and community. The highest-rated types of customization in the organization are the events because people get to meet one another, connect, learn, mastermind, and strategize, and they meet "their people." I am privileged to facilitate world-class connections that turn into all different types of friendships, business partners, and connections.

One to One

These are 1:1 sessions either with team leaders, coaches, or occasionally (depending on the level of the client) myself. Nothing will ever fully replace the power of 1:1 sessions. The human connection is far too important. If you're just getting started as a consultant, a coach, or a trainer, 1:1 is an easy way for you to start and monitor the caliber of your clients and your training.

A quick note to end this chapter: you don't have to start this robust. If you're just starting out, you only really need a few things:

- Expertise (legitimate ways to help someone)

- An offer that makes sense (whether it's information with support or 1:1 engagements)
- A way to get in touch with potential customers and clients

I'm giving you frameworks that will enable you to scale past $10M, $20M, $30M or higher. And when we're talking about those kinds of numbers, it can get more complicated because your business needs to think *for you*. Don't overthink it if you're just getting started.

CHAPTER 9

Tie It All Together

"Well, I don't know if they've heard about this fellow who was going through the cemetery reading all the inscriptions, you know, that's where you find the perfect people, just read the inscriptions. You'll find they're all perfect. One fellow came to one that said, 'As you are now, so once was I. As I am now, you are sure to be. So may I say as here I lie, prepare yourself to follow me.' And somebody had scratched under that, 'To follow you I'm not content until I know which way you went."

- John Wooden

If you take everything from this book and merge it together, it forms a "model."

I've learned from many years of growing and (to be honest) saving businesses that the only way to scale a business safely is by using models. I am constantly testing, tuning, fixing, and updating the models I use. After enough validation, I will put what I know into a framework that will make decisions for the business.

Think about that. I outsource some of my most important business decisions to tested and trusted frameworks. Let me explain.

Your business is an organism, a living, breathing, adapting organism. You want that organism to be smart, strong, resilient, and antifragile. The smartest kinds of businesses use frameworks and models to make decisions. It's easy to fall prey to making an emotional choice when things are difficult. Models use data and, more importantly, organize that data to help you think beyond the problem.

The contents of this book combine to make up one of our models for building consulting and training businesses. This particular model is called the "Codex." There are fifteen models we use, as of now, to build rock-solid (and enjoyable) companies. These models work in all of the following industries because they all deal with the molecular structures of the business:

- Consulting
- Coaching
- Training
- Continued education
- Services
- E-learning

The Phases

Years ago, I was on a phone call with one of my early mentors, Jay Abraham. Jay has impacted my life more than most individuals, both from a marketing point of view and also thinking, problem-solving, and partnerships.

He invented a lot of the materials people treat as commonplace today.

We disagreed, though, on this particular call. Jay is not someone who runs from confrontation. He's earned the right to carry opinions about many things, and he cares deeply for the people in his life, so he was laying it on me.

I believe training and consulting companies can carry intrinsic enterprise value and that they can be sold. I believe this because I've seen it. My venture capital friends are interested in a unique, peculiar business vertical called "Continued Education." They know two things:

1. People are ditching college in favor of "on-the-job learning" and online courses.
2. The customer acquisition costs for their large holdings are getting expensive; attention is in high demand, and there's a large portion of attention-getting gobbled up by these "educators."

A friend of mine had sold his company in the financial education niche. He trained his clients on running significant financial operations using a mixture of online accounting software, hiring virtual assistants, and learning the terminology necessary to read financials.

Who would buy such a business?

I'll tell you — QuickBooks.

All his leads and clients were hole-in-one customers for QuickBooks Online (QBO). Rather than QBO paying *Facebook* or *Google*, or other advertising platforms for the lead, they purchased the customer. This is known as a "strategic" acquisition. The acquisition is not for cash flow (although cash flow will be acquired) but for customer acquisition, economies of scale, and strategic market penetration.

I told Jay that if a company is set up correctly, you can sell it. It doesn't have to be run by the face or the CEO; it can be created in such a way that the value transfer supersedes the contribution of its founder. This takes time, strategy, and above all, consistent execution.

One of the models I've developed is called the "Phases of Business." In my work, I've seen thousands of trainers and consultants. Many of them were marginally successful until we began working together. We have a way of finding the strategic advantages to go hard on to create safe, durable growth.

It's not enough to acquire customers or clients. You must keep them for it to be sustainable. The four phases will help you go from wherever you are right now toward a destination where you are "scalable" and "sellable." The paradox is simple: the things that scale you quickly often remove your sellability. You want to bridge these two things to get both/and rather than either/or.

Sellability is about where value is coming from and how it's being provided.

Scalability is about how attention is secured and when things are installed (speed is often about how much and how fast, whereas scale is about how long and how far).

Of course, we want both! That's why we use the phases of business.

Phase 1: Start-up

The business is brand new (under a year old), and the "message to market" match hasn't been ironed out fully yet. Message-to-market match describes the relationship between the words you say (or write) and how "relatable" those words are to your market.

You can tell a business doesn't have their "message to market" worked out when they're saying things (and selling things) that don't seem appropriate for their customer base. As a business matures, it can change how it communicates to its customers slowly, but a mature business typically has the brand and lingo worked out.

For example, in my company, which trains entrepreneurs on the contents of this book (and all of my other models for business growth), we have a consistent message that is repeated over and over. You know you're in a Phase 1 business (start-up) when you have 1x1x1 on the "Codex." That means you only have one attention platform, one demonstration asset, and one monetization model. That's okay; we all start in Phase 1. The goal is to surround yourself with people and a culture that helps you get to Phase 2 safely and predictably.

Phase 1 is about focus and rapid iteration inside a narrow lane.

Phase 2: Buyback

This phase is marked by your ability to repurchase some of your time for higher-level tasks. In Phase 1, everything tends to find its way back to you. You wear many hats and have many jobs. When you start pushing into Phase 2, you're investing some money into freedom.

So, what does it take to be able to do this? I think in models and frameworks; therefore, I'm going to give you a data-driven answer because I've taken a lot of people into phase 2 territory. The requirements to entirely graduate into Phase 2 are as follows: 3x3x3.

You want three of each pillar of the Codex; three attention platforms, three demonstration assets, and three monetization models. At this point, you should be over the $3 million mark, and phase 2 can take you to $8-10 million. Once you get serious about breaking 8-figures, you must enter Phase 3.

Phase 3: Multiply

Two things happen in Phase 3 that are important. First, you go from a T3 or T2 team to a T1 team. You might enter Phase 3 with a T2 team (great managers), and you've likely secured a T3 team (laborers and front-line workers), but you will not exit Phase 3 without having a solid team of superstar C-level talent. The second change in Phase 3 is when your balance sheet becomes productive.

We have a set of models that help clients run the financials of their businesses. The earlier you start, the more predictable your business will become, and one of the frameworks teaches balance sheets and how to build them. You don't want to use your business for income; you want to use it for wealth building. We aren't stockpiling or hoarding cash at this level; we're multiplying it. Every dollar of free cash flow creates a stream of revenue that multiplies itself. This can be simple cash-flowing assets purchased through the company (such as real estate, buildings, or other businesses). Another form of an asset that many clients secure under our direction is insurance.

Insurance can cash flow, build cash value, and protect you in many scenarios that could be problematic for your business (especially if you have partners). The point is, in Phase 3, your business begins to compound quite quickly. With a T1 team, you're removed from a tier of decisions that used to take your bandwidth. You can build quality at every level; every dollar you save in free cash flow turns into more dollars. A Phase 3 business is hard to break.

To be clear, by the time you enter Phase 2, you can likely sell your business. Once you're in Phase 3, though, you can sell it for more. The whole point of going through the phases is to maximize your enterprise value and increase the personal freedom and wealth you create from your business.

In an all-too-predictable turn of events, most of my clients decide in Phase 3 they no longer want to sell their business! Why would they? If you have something that's paying you millions, multiplying itself, and allowing you to do the work you love (while avoiding the things you don't love), why would you sell it?

You need to sell to a strategic buyer to ensure the "multiple" you sell for is worth the loss of cash flow and leverage your business has created. The multiple is the percentage you will collect in a lump sum for the business. Suppose you have a quickly growing company, with thousands of customers or clients, over 8 figures in revenue, and no concentration risk. In that case, it's not impossible to secure a 5-10x "multiple" on your profits. Phase 3 maximizes this multiple because your team structure reduces concentration risk, and your balance sheet becomes an attractive asset to be acquired with the business's cash flow.

When an owner decides they no longer wish to sell their business in this phase, we call this an "amortized exit." That's another model for another day, but in essence, it means this: the owner has replaced a "lump sum" exit with a long-term exit that will pay them much more in the long run.

Phase 4: Harvest

This is the phase of business everyone dreams about.

When you started your company, you likely envisioned a Phase 4 business. Even if you didn't think as big as a Phase 4 business, you wanted a Phase 4 business stylistically. It is marked by the following:

- Work if you want, don't work if you don't want.
- Enjoy 100% of the work, and outsource anything you don't enjoy.
- All financial needs met and exceeded.
- Personal fulfillment (not just working for money, you love the work itself).
- Your legacy is being built and enhanced because of the business.

You can get all these things in Phase 3, but Phase 4 is when you begin to enjoy them. The business isn't reliant on you anymore, so you can sell it if you want to. You can sell it to an outside buyer or sell part of it to employees via stock options and bonuses.

A Phase 4 business has plenty of problems, but you are well-supported enough to never have to face them alone. In fact, facing them (and solving them) is half the fun. A Phase 4 business is something you love to own, a wonderful business you aren't desperate to get rid of.

However, because of how you set it up, it's always "for sale." When you do sell, you'll sell for the largest multiple and the most lump sum cash you can; it will fetch the attention of large firms that respect not only what you've built but your competency in building it.

Why the Codex Exists and How I Built It

Now you know how important this book is. It's not just about scaling your business; it's about scaling it in a way that secures maximum freedom and durability along the way.

I built the Codex because I have grown a lot of multi-7 and 8-figure businesses. People are usually looking for ways to get more clients and more revenue, and at the end of the day, two things matter more than all the rest:

- Not how much you make but how much you keep.
- Not how fast you grow but how long you can stay there.

If you can maximize your staying power while continuously and conscientiously improving your profits, you are on the right path. We specialize in taking businesses from Phases 1 and 2 to Phases 3 and 4. Look at your business holistically right now, and answer these questions:

- Is my business using at least three forms of attention, demonstration, and monetization?
- Do I have consistently 20% year-over-year growth from the last three years?
- If I, as the founder, disappeared for six months, would my business grow or shrink?
- If no revenue came in for 12 months, is my balance sheet strong enough to handle it without layoffs or slowdowns?
- Do I have a pipeline of new products coming out to offer value to my market each quarter?
- Does my team efficiently produce my revenues, or is there a concentration risk on me as the producer?

I wrote this book to help you fix these problems using models and frameworks that have withstood the test of thousands of clients. Each year, they get better and more effective.

CHAPTER 10

What To Do Next

"If you chase money desperately in the earnest belief that you can never be happy without it and seriously think that the chase is a meaningful occupation, I doubt very much you will succeed." - Felix Dennis

One of the most important decisions you will make in your business is who you trust to help you grow your company. The world is filling up with new "experts" who have never built businesses. Every day there's a new program coming online. You must thoroughly vet the voices you trust to work on your mind.

If someone lacks the experience, they will transfer that cost to you. Information is the data, but wisdom is the proper ability to make great decisions that maximize your upside and minimize your downside. My goal has always been simple: create a legacy by helping people. The mission statement for my training company, The Wealth Consultant, is to unlock and monetize human experience and expertise.

My strategy for doing so has been simple. I don't want the most money award; I want the most value award. Pound for pound, whoever transfers the most value, wins. However, value isn't just about volume;

it's about duration. I've been doing this for a long time, and hopefully, you've found tremendous utility by investing your time in reading this book.

If you are looking for more, consider the following free resources for consistent training & information…

Podcast

I published a podcast called "THE GOOD LIFE w/Taylor Welch." Each week, I share pieces of event content, private consulting sessions, and behind-the-scenes training you can't find anywhere else. Check it out at taylorawelch.com/podcast

Blog

When I have something to say, I usually publish a piece of content around it. You can read other pieces of writing from me by visiting taylorawelch.com/blog

YouTube

Each week I publish videos breaking down the complexities of my work. I grow businesses for a living, and I get to see some of the best (and worst) kinds of companies. If you enjoy business & life philosophy, blended together in one simple place — the channel is a good bet. YouTube.com/taylorawelch for that

Social Media

I publish consistently on Facebook, Twitter, and Instagram. Search "Taylor Welch" or user @taylorawelch and you should find me.

Specific Support

If you're building a training, coaching, or consulting company, and would like support specifically tuned to your business — you can view a treasure trove of content at WealthyConsultant.com. We publish a podcast just for business owners like you and have a suite of products and programs that will help accelerate your journey toward a secure, durable, *enjoyable* business.

DOWNLOAD YOUR FREE GIFTS

Just to say thanks for buying and reading my book, I would like to give you a few free bonus gifts, no strings attached!

Download Your Free Gifts Now:

I appreciate your interest in my book, and value your feedback as it helps me improve future versions. I would appreciate it if you could leave your invaluable review on Amazon.com with your feedback. Thank you!

Made in the USA
Las Vegas, NV
08 November 2024

11374608R10073